FROM FARM TO DINNER TABLE

Food's Great Journey

by Doris Licameli

Table of Contents

Introduction

It's time to eat. Dad has made a tasty meal. He used **fresh** food to make a healthy dinner. Later, there will be a magnificent apple pie for dessert. It's made from a prize recipe with lots of ingredients. This is Dad's masterpiece!

Eating fresh foods is important. They have **vitamins** that help keep us healthy. But where does fresh food come from? How does it get to our homes?

↻ We need fresh healthful food every day.

Chapter 1 On the Farm

Most food comes from farms. Farmers plant seeds for fruit, vegetables, and cereal crops. They **harvest** these crops when they are ripe. Chickens are raised on farms too. And some farmers raise cattle for meat and milk products. There are thousands of farms across the United States.

But most people don't live near farms. The food has to travel to reach them.

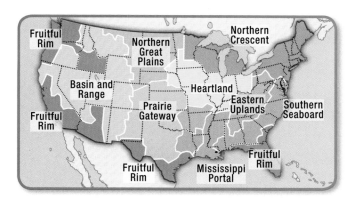

This map shows the farm areas in the United States.

FAST FACT There are about 77,000 farms in Wisconsin alone. Each farm provides food for 135 people.

🎧 Farmers often sell their fruits and vegetables themselves.

Food did not always travel far from farms. Travel took a long time. There were no roads, only bumpy dirt trails. And the only way to get around was with a wagon pulled by a horse.

The Apple Man

Apples came to North America with the early settlers. Later, Native Americans planted apple trees. John Chapman helped spread apple trees across the country. He planted apple seeds wherever he went. He is now known as "Johnny Appleseed."

Then things began to change. New roads were built. Steamboats appeared on the rivers. Railroad trains were introduced. Many towns and cities were connected. Now food could travel farther from the farms.

In 1869 the first ⊃ transcontinental rail line was completed across the United States.

⍁ Steamboats are still used to ship food to many parts of the world.

Chapter 2 Trucks On the Job

Motor trucks came in the early 1900s. They replaced slow horse-drawn farm wagons. But early trucks had no doors or roofs, so rain could be a problem.

⌒ Most early trucks didn't have any headlights to see in the dark. Drivers used oil lamps at night.

 FAST FACT In 1916, it took 31 days for a truck to travel from Seattle to New York City.

↷ These refrigerator trucks carry fruits, vegetables, and meat at the right temperature.

Modern trucks are big and fast. Some have 18 wheels. Many trucks are huge **refrigerators** on wheels. Apples, beef, and milk stay fresh as they travel. They arrive fast, without spoiling.

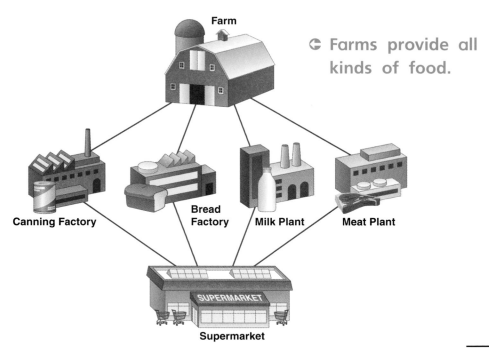

↶ Farms provide all kinds of food.

Farm

Canning Factory

Bread Factory

Milk Plant

Meat Plant

Supermarket

Chapter 3 Trains, Ships, Planes

Many people were very happy when steam locomotives were invented. Locomotives could go 20 miles (32 km) per hour.

Farmers welcomed railroads. Now trains could deliver food in a week instead of a month. People living in towns far from farms were able to buy fruits and vegetables all year long.

Miles of Freight	
A ton-mile is one ton carried one mile. One ton is 2,000 pounds (907kg).	
Year	**Ton-miles of Freight Carried**
1860	3 billion
1900	141 billion
2002	$1\frac{1}{2}$ trillion

Label It

Labels were put on fresh and canned food. These labels helped shippers to keep track of what they were shipping.

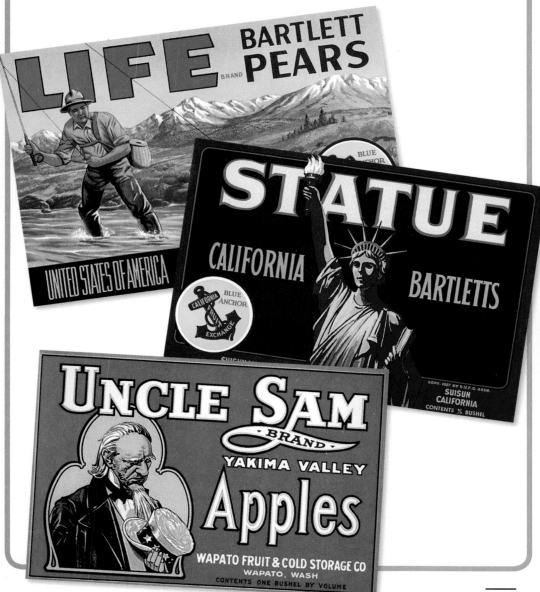

Ships became another way to move food easily. A shipping container is a big metal box. The usual size is 20 feet (6 m) long and 8 feet ($2\frac{2}{5}$ m) wide. That can be about the size of a classroom. The containers hold huge amounts of goods. And they can be moved from a truck to a train to a ship quickly.

⊙ Container shipping speeds the loading and unloading of freight trains.

FAST FACT There can be as many as 5,000 containers on a single ship.

Refrigerated containers keep food fresh. Most containers get stacked like blocks on the deck of a ship. But these containers need power to stay cool. They are set in a place close to electric outlets.

↻ This is a container ship.

The Banana Boat

In the late 1890s ships carrying bananas were painted white. It was thought that white would reflect the hot tropical sun and keep the bananas at the right temperature. These ships were called the Great White Fleet.

Airplanes are another way to move food quickly and safely. Airplanes can fly hundreds of miles in an hour. Shipping by air costs more than by land. Only some foods, like pineapples, come to us this way. They must be picked fully ripe and be rushed to **markets**.

Fresh fish and seafood are flown on airplanes too. That's the fastest way to get them to markets.

◑ This fresh fish market sells and ships thousands of pounds of fish daily.

Conclusion

There is nothing better than fresh farm foods, but most people don't live on farms. So the next best thing is to move food fast. Food doesn't lose its vitamins when it comes to market quickly.

Now people are looking for new ways to transport food. What do you think will be next?

↻ Today, fresh vegetables are available in local markets.

Progress in Travel

Propeller Airplane 1903

1800   **1900**

1807
Steamboat

1829
Steam Locomotive

1892
Gasoline Auto

Glossary

fresh *(FRESH)* newly done, made, or gathered *(page 2)*

harvest *(HAHR-vist)* the gathering in of a crop when it is ripe *(page 3)*

market *(MAHR-kit)* a place where goods are sold *(page 12)*

refrigerator *(ri-FRIJ-uh-ray-tuhr)* an appliance, box, or room with a cooling system, used to keep food from spoiling *(page 7)*

vitamin *(VIGH-tuh-min)* one of a group of substances needed in small amounts for the health and the normal working of the body *(page 2)*

Index

Comprehension Check

Summarize

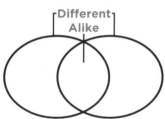

Different
Alike

Use a Venn diagram to compare and contrast the way trucks move food with the way airplanes move food. Then use the diagram to summarize the book.

Think and Compare

1. Reread pages 6-7. How have food trucks changed over time? *(Compare and Contrast)*

2. What are some of your favorite meals and recipes? Why do you like them? *(Evaluate)*

3. Why do you think the cost of food goes up when there is too little rain? *(Synthesize)*